MAD LIBS®

LOVE THE EARTH
MAD LIBS

by Corey Powell

MAD LIBS
An Imprint of Penguin Random House LLC, New York

Mad Libs format and text copyright © 2021 by Penguin Random House LLC.
All rights reserved.

Concept created by Roger Price & Leonard Stern

Cover illustration by Scott Brooks

Published by Mad Libs,
an imprint of Penguin Random House LLC, New York.
Printed in the USA.

Visit us online at www.penguinrandomhouse.com.

ISBN 9780593224137
3 5 7 9 10 8 6 4

MAD LIBS

INSTRUCTIONS

MAD LIBS® is a game for people who don't like games! It can be played by one, two, three, four, or forty.

• RIDICULOUSLY SIMPLE DIRECTIONS

In this tablet you will find stories containing blank spaces where words are left out. One player, the READER, selects one of these stories. The READER does not tell anyone what the story is about. Instead, he/she asks the other players, the WRITERS, to give him/her words. These words are used to fill in the blank spaces in the story.

• TO PLAY

The READER asks each WRITER in turn to call out a word—an adjective or a noun or whatever the space calls for—and uses them to fill in the blank spaces in the story. The result is a MAD LIBS® game.

When the READER then reads the completed MAD LIBS® game to the other players, they will discover that they have written a story that is fantastic, screamingly funny, shocking, silly, crazy, or just plain dumb—depending upon which words each WRITER called out.

• EXAMPLE (Before and After)

"_____!" he said _____
           EXCLAMATION   ADVERB

as he jumped into his convertible _____ and
                                            NOUN

drove off with his _____ wife.
                          ADJECTIVE

"_____OUCH_____!" he said _____HAPPILY_____
           EXCLAMATION   ADVERB

as he jumped into his convertible _____CAT_____ and
                                            NOUN

drove off with his _____BRAVE_____ wife.
                          ADJECTIVE

In case you have forgotten what adjectives, adverbs, nouns, and verbs are, here is a quick review:

An ADJECTIVE describes something or somebody. *Lumpy, soft, ugly, messy,* and *short* are adjectives.

An ADVERB tells how something is done. It modifies a verb and usually ends in "ly." *Modestly, stupidly, greedily,* and *carefully* are adverbs.

A NOUN is the name of a person, place, or thing. *Sidewalk, umbrella, bridle, bathtub,* and *nose* are nouns.

A VERB is an action word. *Run, pitch, jump,* and *swim* are verbs. Put the verbs in past tense if the directions say PAST TENSE. *Ran, pitched, jumped,* and *swam* are verbs in the past tense.

When we ask for A PLACE, we mean any sort of place: a country or city (*Spain, Cleveland*) or a room (*bathroom, kitchen*).

An EXCLAMATION or SILLY WORD is any sort of funny sound, gasp, grunt, or outcry, like *Wow!, Ouch!, Whomp!, Ick!,* and *Gadzooks!*

When we ask for specific words, like a NUMBER, a COLOR, an ANIMAL, or a PART OF THE BODY, we mean a word that is one of those things, like *seven, blue, horse,* or *head.*

When we ask for a PLURAL, it means more than one. For example, *cat* pluralized is *cats.*

MAD LIBS® is fun to play with friends, but you can also play it by yourself! To begin with, DO NOT look at the story on the page below. Fill in the blanks on this page with the words called for. Then, using the words you have selected, fill in the blank spaces in the story.

Now you've created your own hilarious MAD LIBS® game!

MY VERY FIRST EARTH DAY

NUMBER _____

ADJECTIVE _____

PART OF THE BODY (PLURAL) _____

COLOR _____

VERB _____

VERB _____

NOUN _____

ADJECTIVE _____

ADJECTIVE _____

PERSON IN ROOM _____

EXCLAMATION _____

ARTICLE OF CLOTHING _____

PLURAL NOUN _____

VERB _____

VERB _____

A PLACE _____

ADJECTIVE _____

ADJECTIVE _____

MAD LIBS®

MY VERY FIRST EARTH DAY

Three! Two! _____! Go! It's time for my very first
__NUMBER__

Earth Day. I'm so _____! I can't wait to sink my bare
__ADJECTIVE__

_____ into the _____ grass and take some
__PART OF THE BODY (PLURAL)__   __COLOR__

time to just _____. I decided I just can't _____ at
__VERB__   __VERB__

home on my _____ all day anymore. Instead, I'm gonna
__NOUN__

make the world a/an _____ place. I mean, Earth is already
__ADJECTIVE__

_____, but me and my best friend, _____, will
__ADJECTIVE__   __PERSON IN ROOM__

make it even more amazing. _____! So, I'm going to put
__EXCLAMATION__

on my favorite vegan _____ and my best nontoxic
__ARTICLE OF CLOTHING__

_____, so I can look great while I _____ the
__PLURAL NOUN__   __VERB__

world. In fact, I'm gonna _____ the Earth so hard that there
__VERB__

won't even be time to take a selfie in front of (the) _____. It's
__A PLACE__

gonna be the most _____ day ever. Because you know what
__ADJECTIVE__

they say, a good planet is _____ to find!
__ADJECTIVE__

MAD LIBS® is fun to play with friends, but you can also play it by yourself! To begin with, DO NOT look at the story on the page below. Fill in the blanks on this page with the words called for. Then, using the words you have selected, fill in the blank spaces in the story.

Now you've created your own hilarious MAD LIBS® game!

A POEM FOR MOTHER EARTH

NOUN _____

VERB _____

PLURAL NOUN _____

A PLACE _____

ADJECTIVE _____

VERB _____

ADJECTIVE _____

VERB _____

ADJECTIVE _____

PLURAL NOUN _____

ADJECTIVE _____

SOMETHING ALIVE _____

PLURAL NOUN _____

NOUN _____

ADJECTIVE _____

A PLACE _____

MAD LIBS
A POEM FOR MOTHER EARTH

The only _____ that has any worth
NOUN

is the one that helps _____ Mother Earth.
VERB

Her _____ are so pretty,
PLURAL NOUN

from (the) _____ to every city.
A PLACE

There's no _____ place to _____ than our
ADJECTIVE   VERB

_____ sphere,
ADJECTIVE

so we need to _____ to make sure it's always here.
VERB

We can't leave our planet _____ and defaced,
ADJECTIVE

or covered in _____ and _____ waste.
PLURAL NOUN   ADJECTIVE

There are things every _____ can do
SOMETHING ALIVE

to make better _____ for me and you.
PLURAL NOUN

That's why _____ Day is a/an _____ reminder
NOUN   ADJECTIVE

to treat (the) _____ a little bit kinder.
A PLACE

MAD LIBS® is fun to play with friends, but you can also play it by yourself! To begin with, DO NOT look at the story on the page below. Fill in the blanks on this page with the words called for. Then, using the words you have selected, fill in the blank spaces in the story.

Now you've created your own hilarious MAD LIBS® game!

HISTORY OF EARTH DAY

VERB ENDING IN "ING" _____

ADJECTIVE _____

NUMBER _____

TYPE OF LIQUID _____

VERB (PAST TENSE) _____

A PLACE _____

NOUN _____

ADJECTIVE _____

VERB (PAST TENSE) _____

PLURAL NOUN _____

VERB ENDING IN "ING" _____

OCCUPATION (PLURAL) _____

VERB _____

TYPE OF EVENT _____

VERB ENDING IN "ING" _____

ADJECTIVE _____

ADJECTIVE _____

OCCUPATION _____

MAD LIBS®

HISTORY OF EARTH DAY

Some of you may be _____ about how Earth Day first
                        VERB ENDING IN "ING"

came to be. Well, it's a pretty _____ story that goes all the
                                  ADJECTIVE

way back to 1969, which is over _____ years ago. It all started
                                 NUMBER

when there was a horrible _____ spill in Santa Barbara,
                          TYPE OF LIQUID

California. Oil _____ all over (the) _____ .
               VERB (PAST TENSE)   A PLACE

It was a huge environmental _____ , and people were very
                            NOUN

_____ about it. So, a few organizers _____
ADJECTIVE   VERB (PAST TENSE)

together to fight for new _____ to help keep disasters
                          PLURAL NOUN

like this from ever _____ again. Soon after, these
                    VERB ENDING IN "ING"

_____ were ready to _____ others, so they
OCCUPATION (PLURAL)   VERB

started the first Earth Day _____ , which was all about
                            TYPE OF EVENT

_____ the planet. Now, it's a/an _____ festival
VERB ENDING IN "ING"   ADJECTIVE

where all types of _____ people come together to learn
                   ADJECTIVE

about how to be an environmental _____ .
                                 OCCUPATION

MAD LIBS® is fun to play with friends, but you can also play it by yourself! To begin with, DO NOT look at the story on the page below. Fill in the blanks on this page with the words called for. Then, using the words you have selected, fill in the blank spaces in the story.

Now you've created your own hilarious MAD LIBS® game!

GOING GREEN AND GROOVY

VERB ENDING IN "ING" _____

TYPE OF LIQUID _____

NOUN _____

TYPE OF CONTAINER _____

TYPE OF FOOD _____

COLOR _____

ADVERB _____

ADJECTIVE _____

TYPE OF FOOD _____

ADJECTIVE _____

VERB _____

A PLACE _____

ADVERB _____

VERB _____

ADJECTIVE _____

MAD LIBS®
GOING GREEN
AND GROOVY

Giselle and Marisela are getting ready for an eco-vacation and are

_____ what to pack:

VERB ENDING IN "ING"

Giselle: Did you pack my eco-friendly _____ bottle and

TYPE OF LIQUID

my straw made out of _____ ?

NOUN

Marisela: Yep! They're already in our _____ made of

TYPE OF CONTAINER

recycled _____ bags.

TYPE OF FOOD

Giselle: That reminds me. I forgot the _____ crystals. If we

COLOR

don't have them with us, things could go _____ wrong.

ADVERB

Oh, and did you remember the _____ nectar? You know if

ADJECTIVE

I have too much _____ , I get really _____ .

TYPE OF FOOD _ADJECTIVE_

Marisela: I'd never _____ that. (The) _____

VERB _A PLACE_

is in retrograde and that's not something you should ever take

_____ .

ADVERB

Giselle: I _____ you. Let's hum a few rounds of "om"

VERB

before we go, so our vibes stay really _____ . Ommmmmmm!

ADJECTIVE

From LOVE THE EARTH MAD LIBS® • Copyright © 2021 by Penguin Random House LLC.

MAD LIBS® is fun to play with friends, but you can also play it by yourself! To begin with, DO NOT look at the story on the page below. Fill in the blanks on this page with the words called for. Then, using the words you have selected, fill in the blank spaces in the story.

Now you've created your own hilarious MAD LIBS® game!

SPRING HAS SPRUNG!

PLURAL NOUN _____

ADJECTIVE _____

CELEBRITY _____

NOUN _____

NUMBER _____

NOUN _____

ADJECTIVE _____

VERB _____

PLURAL NOUN _____

SOMETHING ALIVE (PLURAL) _____

VERB ENDING IN "ING" _____

PLURAL NOUN _____

PLURAL NOUN _____

ADJECTIVE _____

EXCLAMATION _____

NOUN _____

ARTICLE OF CLOTHING _____

MAD LIBS®

SPRING HAS SPRUNG!

Hello. Professor von Reuseinit here, with a few fun scientific

_____ about Earth Day. It's all very _____, or at
PLURAL NOUN   ADJECTIVE

least the famous astronomer _____ would think so! Did
                              CELEBRITY

you know Earth Day happens on the same _____ every
                                          NOUN

_____ days? This day is called the spring equinox, and it is
NUMBER

when the visible _____ is exactly above the equator. Pretty
                  NOUN

cool, huh? It's a very _____ time because it symbolizes growth
                        ADJECTIVE

and the first day of spring. And who doesn't _____ this
                                              VERB

beautiful time of the year? After all, as they say, April _____
                                                          PLURAL NOUN

bring May _____! That's probably why so many
          SOMETHING ALIVE (PLURAL)

people enjoy _____ Earth Day! It's when the
              VERB ENDING IN "ING"

_____ get longer and the _____ start to appear
PLURAL NOUN   PLURAL NOUN

on those _____ trees. So, hip hip _____ for
          ADJECTIVE   EXCLAMATION

spring. It's time to put on your mineral-based _____-block,
                                                NOUN

take off your _____, and bask in the glorious renewal
               ARTICLE OF CLOTHING

of planet Earth.

MAD LIBS® is fun to play with friends, but you can also play it by yourself! To begin with, DO NOT look at the story on the page below. Fill in the blanks on this page with the words called for. Then, using the words you have selected, fill in the blank spaces in the story.

Now you've created your own hilarious MAD LIBS® game!

NO PLANES, NO TRAINS, NO AUTOMOBILES

ADJECTIVE _____

VEHICLE _____

TYPE OF LIQUID _____

ADJECTIVE _____

ADJECTIVE _____

NOUN _____

PART OF THE BODY (PLURAL) _____

PLURAL NOUN _____

VERB _____

ADJECTIVE _____

PLURAL NOUN _____

VERB _____

VERB _____

VEHICLE _____

NOUN _____

VERB (PAST TENSE) _____

EXCLAMATION _____

MAD LIBS
NO PLANES, NO TRAINS,
NO AUTOMOBILES

Rudy and Kevin are determined to find the most environmentally

_____ way to get to work.
   ADJECTIVE

Rudy: Hey, man, I can't drive a/an _____ that runs on
                                       VEHICLE

_____ . That's so not _____ .
TYPE OF LIQUID   ADJECTIVE

Kevin: Diggin' your whole _____ vibe, man. We've
                                    ADJECTIVE

gotta treat Mother Nature with _____ and use our
                                    NOUN

_____ to get there.
PART OF THE BODY (PLURAL)

Rudy: Or we could, like, build a bicycle out of used _____
                                    PLURAL NOUN

and then _____ across town.
        VERB

Kevin: Dude! I have a/an _____ idea. We can just put eco-
                      ADJECTIVE

friendly, petroleum-free _____ on our feet and then
                      PLURAL NOUN

_____ the whole way.
   VERB

Rudy: Totally, or maybe we could just _____ really hard and,
                      VERB

like, manifest a new type of _____ that, like, runs on
                    VEHICLE

_____ or something.
   NOUN

Kevin: Magical! Man, you've got this all _____ out.
                      VERB (PAST TENSE)

_____ .
EXCLAMATION

MAD LIBS® is fun to play with friends, but you can also play it by yourself! To begin with, DO NOT look at the story on the page below. Fill in the blanks on this page with the words called for. Then, using the words you have selected, fill in the blank spaces in the story.

Now you've created your own hilarious MAD LIBS® game!

EARTH DAY RULES!

TYPE OF EVENT _____

ADJECTIVE _____

NOUN _____

ARTICLE OF CLOTHING _____

PART OF THE BODY (PLURAL) _____

VERB ENDING IN "ING" _____

TYPE OF BUILDING _____

NOUN _____

ADJECTIVE _____

NOUN _____

VERB _____

NOUN _____

ADJECTIVE _____

ADVERB _____

VERB _____

ANIMAL _____

VERB _____

VERB _____

MAD LIBS

EARTH DAY RULES!

This year's Earth Day _____ has a few _____
                        TYPE OF EVENT   ADJECTIVE

rules:

- To avoid getting a/an _____ -burn, wear a hat
                            NOUN

  and long-sleeve _____ that covers your
                        ARTICLE OF CLOTHING

  _____.
  PART OF THE BODY (PLURAL)

- No _____ on your cell phone in the meditation
       VERB ENDING IN "ING"

  _____. Fellow Earth Dayers are on a/an _____
  TYPE OF BUILDING   NOUN

  to enlightenment and must not have _____ vibrations
                                          ADJECTIVE

  in their aura.

- Exude positive _____. So, make sure to _____
                    NOUN   VERB

  at everyone who crosses your _____.
                                    NOUN

- If someone is having a/an _____ day, don't just
                                ADJECTIVE

  _____ run away. Make sure they know you _____
    ADVERB   VERB

  them.

- Karma can be a real _____, so _____ others the
                        ANIMAL   VERB

  way you would want them to _____ you.
                                  VERB

MAD LIBS® is fun to play with friends, but you can also play it by yourself! To begin with, DO NOT look at the story on the page below. Fill in the blanks on this page with the words called for. Then, using the words you have selected, fill in the blank spaces in the story.

Now you've created your own hilarious MAD LIBS® game!

MY MEDITATION

ADJECTIVE _____

CELEBRITY _____

NOUN _____

VERB _____

NUMBER _____

VERB _____

A PLACE _____

VERB ENDING IN "ING" _____

NUMBER _____

PART OF THE BODY _____

TYPE OF LIQUID _____

VERB ENDING IN "ING" _____

NOUN _____

COLOR _____

ADVERB _____

NOUN _____

ADVERB _____

EXCLAMATION _____

MAD LIBS®

MY MEDITATION

This _____ meditation will help you feel as centered
         ADJECTIVE

as the great spiritual leader _____. First, take a deep
                                  CELEBRITY

_____ in. Now, let it out slowly and _____ your
    NOUN   VERB

body. Repeat this for the next _____ minutes as you
                                      NUMBER

_____ to the sound of my voice. Next, go to that happy
    VERB

_____ in your mind and just be. When you're done
      A PLACE

_____, take _____ fingers and place them on
VERB ENDING IN "ING"   NUMBER

your _____. Feel the _____ flowing easily
      PART OF THE BODY   TYPE OF LIQUID

through your veins. Remember to keep _____ as your
                                        VERB ENDING IN "ING"

_____ sinks further and further into relaxation. Now,
      NOUN

imagine your _____ chakra is _____ pulsing, like
               COLOR   ADVERB

the flame of a/an _____ dancing in the wind. Stay with it.
                     NOUN

Then, exhale _____ and say _____.
               ADVERB   EXCLAMATION

MAD LIBS® is fun to play with friends, but you can also play it by yourself! To begin with, DO NOT look at the story on the page below. Fill in the blanks on this page with the words called for. Then, using the words you have selected, fill in the blank spaces in the story.

Now you've created your own hilarious MAD LIBS® game!

YUMMY YUMMY
IN MY THIRD CHAKRA

PART OF THE BODY _____

PERSON IN ROOM _____

COLOR _____

TYPE OF FOOD _____

PLURAL NOUN _____

NUMBER _____

ADJECTIVE _____

SOMETHING ALIVE _____

TYPE OF LIQUID _____

VERB _____

TYPE OF CONTAINER _____

NOUN _____

COLOR _____

VERB _____

ADJECTIVE _____

PART OF THE BODY _____

TYPE OF LIQUID _____

NOUN _____

MAD LIBS®
YUMMY YUMMY
IN MY THIRD CHAKRA

The best organic recipes come from the _____ , and
PART OF THE BODY

_____ knows a really good one called the _____
PERSON IN ROOM   COLOR

groovy smoothie.

Ingredients:

- One Reiki-blessed, organic _____ , sprinkled with
  TYPE OF FOOD

  gluten-free _____
  PLURAL NOUN

- Three _____-leaf clovers, borrowed from a/an
  NUMBER

  _____ farmer
  ADJECTIVE

- _____ clippings cured in a barrel of _____
  SOMETHING ALIVE   TYPE OF LIQUID

Directions:

Gently _____ all the ingredients into a/an _____
VERB   TYPE OF CONTAINER

made of _____ and humanely sourced iron until the broth
NOUN

turns _____ . Direct your energy into the pot until you
COLOR

see it _____ . Add in some _____ intentions
VERB   ADJECTIVE

and a dash of salt. When it feels right, mix everything with your

_____ and add alkaline _____ . Season with
PART OF THE BODY   TYPE OF LIQUID

_____ to taste.
NOUN

MAD LIBS® is fun to play with friends, but you can also play it by yourself! To begin with, DO NOT look at the story on the page below. Fill in the blanks on this page with the words called for. Then, using the words you have selected, fill in the blank spaces in the story.

Now you've created your own hilarious MAD LIBS® game!

OINKS AND NEIGHS

VERB _____

PERSON IN ROOM _____

ANIMAL _____

PART OF THE BODY _____

VERB (PAST TENSE) _____

ANIMAL _____

TYPE OF FOOD _____

TYPE OF LIQUID _____

ARTICLE OF CLOTHING _____

PART OF THE BODY _____

ADJECTIVE _____

NUMBER _____

VEHICLE _____

ADJECTIVE _____

CITY _____

ADJECTIVE _____

MAD LIBS®

OINKS AND NEIGHS

Welcome to my wildlife rescue center, where the animals do more

than _____!
    VERB

- Our first pet friend is _____ the _____ . He
                        PERSON IN ROOM   ANIMAL

  loves to have his _____ _____ every
                    PART OF THE BODY   VERB (PAST TENSE)

  chance he gets.

- This is Genevieve the _____ . Her favorite meal is
                        ANIMAL

  _____ mixed with a dash of _____ .
   TYPE OF FOOD   TYPE OF LIQUID

- Henry the turtle likes to wear a/an _____ on
                                      ARTICLE OF CLOTHING

  his _____ because it keeps him _____ .
      PART OF THE BODY   ADJECTIVE

- Cluckety the chicken can count to _____ and drive
                                     NUMBER

  a/an _____ with just her beak. Last time she took a/an
        VEHICLE

  _____ ride, she ended up all the way in _____ .
   ADJECTIVE   CITY

  She's one _____ bird.
             ADJECTIVE

MAD LIBS® is fun to play with friends, but you can also play it by yourself! To begin with, DO NOT look at the story on the page below. Fill in the blanks on this page with the words called for. Then, using the words you have selected, fill in the blank spaces in the story.

Now you've created your own hilarious MAD LIBS® game!

YOGATTA DO IT

OCCUPATION (PLURAL) _____

PART OF THE BODY _____

NOUN _____

VERB _____

PERSON IN ROOM _____

VERB _____

ADJECTIVE _____

PART OF THE BODY _____

VERB ENDING IN "ING" _____

PART OF THE BODY _____

ANIMAL _____

VERB _____

ADJECTIVE _____

SOMETHING ALIVE _____

VERB _____

ADVERB _____

NOUN _____

NUMBER _____

MAD LIBS®

YOGATTA DO IT

Namaste, my dedicated _____ . It's time to expand
OCCUPATION (PLURAL)

your mind and _____ . Reach your hands up to the
PART OF THE BODY

_____ , take a deep breath, and _____ until you feel
NOUN   VERB

the burn. Hold the pose and turn your head toward _____
PERSON IN ROOM

and inhale. What do you _____ ? Does it make you feel
VERB

_____ ? Feel the energy in your _____ and
ADJECTIVE   PART OF THE BODY

then send it back by _____ it through your
VERB ENDING IN "ING"

_____ . When you're done, change your pose to
PART OF THE BODY

downward-facing _____ . Remember, it's still important to
ANIMAL

_____ . Breathe out and then relax in _____
VERB   ADJECTIVE

_____ pose. When you're ready, put your weight on the
SOMETHING ALIVE

tips of your toes and _____ them _____ . Now reach
VERB   ADVERB

for the sky again, put your hands in _____ position, and
NOUN

say "om" _____ times. Namaste.
NUMBER

MAD LIBS® is fun to play with friends, but you can also play it by yourself! To begin with, DO NOT look at the story on the page below. Fill in the blanks on this page with the words called for. Then, using the words you have selected, fill in the blank spaces in the story.

Now you've created your own hilarious MAD LIBS® game!

SEPARATE, PEOPLE!

OCCUPATION _____

ADJECTIVE _____

ADVERB _____

NOUN _____

TYPE OF CONTAINER _____

TYPE OF VEHICLE _____

VERB _____

A PLACE _____

EXCLAMATION _____

NOUN _____

VERB ENDING IN "ING" _____

VERB _____

PLURAL NOUN _____

NOUN _____

VERB _____

TYPE OF CONTAINER _____

PART OF THE BODY _____

MAD LIBS®

SEPARATE, PEOPLE!

A/An _____ tells a new middle-school student how to
OCCUPATION

separate trash from recycling.

Monitor: The first thing you need to know is that recycling is very

_____ , and you should do it _____ .
ADJECTIVE   ADVERB

Boy: So, does that mean I should put my _____ into
NOUN

a/an _____ ?
TYPE OF CONTAINER

Monitor: Nope, if you do that, the _____ won't be able to
TYPE OF VEHICLE

_____ it to (the) _____ .
VERB   A PLACE

Boy: _____ , I sure don't want that to happen.
EXCLAMATION

I should put my plate made of _____ into the blue
NOUN

_____ bin.
VERB ENDING IN "ING"

Monitor: Right! And then you should _____ your uneaten
VERB

fruit and _____ into the compost _____ .
PLURAL NOUN   NOUN

Boy: That means that everything else should _____ into
VERB

the trash _____ .
TYPE OF CONTAINER

Monitor: Way to use your _____ to make the right
PART OF THE BODY

choices!

MAD LIBS® is fun to play with friends, but you can also play it by yourself! To begin with, DO NOT look at the story on the page below. Fill in the blanks on this page with the words called for. Then, using the words you have selected, fill in the blank spaces in the story.

Now you've created your own hilarious MAD LIBS® game!

SONG FOR MAMA EARTH

VERB _____

COLOR _____

ADJECTIVE _____

PART OF THE BODY _____

VERB _____

NOUN _____

ADVERB _____

ADJECTIVE _____

NOUN _____

VERB _____

VERB (PAST TENSE) _____

NOUN _____

VERB _____

NOUN _____

SILLY WORD _____

SILLY WORD _____

VERB _____

MAD LIBS®

SONG FOR MAMA EARTH

I _____ this big _____ ball called Mother Earth;
　　　　VERB　　　　　　　　　COLOR

she's taken _____ care of me since birth.
　　　　　　　ADJECTIVE

My _____ skips a beat
　　PART OF THE BODY

whenever her waves _____ over my feet.
　　　　　　　　　　　VERB

And a/an _____ comes to my eye
　　　　　　NOUN

whenever I stare _____ at her _____ sky.
　　　　　　　　　ADVERB　　　　　　ADJECTIVE

Her _____-tops are so pretty,
　　NOUN

they inspired me to _____ this ditty.
　　　　　　　　　　VERB

And so, I _____ here to say,
　　　　　VERB (PAST TENSE)

protect this _____ each day!
　　　　　　　NOUN

She sure does _____ us a lot,
　　　　　　　VERB

and she's the only _____ we've got!
　　　　　　　　　NOUN

Sha-la-la-la- _____ - _____ -hey-hey!
　　　　　　　SILLY WORD　　SILLY WORD

Let's _____ Mother Earth in every way!
　　　VERB

MAD LIBS® is fun to play with friends, but you can also play it by yourself! To begin with, DO NOT look at the story on the page below. Fill in the blanks on this page with the words called for. Then, using the words you have selected, fill in the blank spaces in the story.

Now you've created your own hilarious MAD LIBS® game!

MY URBAN FARM

VERB _____

NOUN _____

VERB _____

ADJECTIVE _____

A PLACE _____

PLURAL NOUN _____

VERB _____

TYPE OF LIQUID _____

VERB _____

ADJECTIVE _____

SOMETHING ALIVE (PLURAL) _____

ANIMAL (PLURAL) _____

ADJECTIVE _____

VERB (PAST TENSE) _____

VERB (PAST TENSE) _____

COLOR _____

ANIMAL (PLURAL) _____

VERB ENDING IN "ING" _____

MAD LIBS

MY URBAN FARM

Here's how to _____ a beautiful organic garden in the
VERB

big _____ :
NOUN

1. _____ your seeds from a/an _____ _____
   VERB   ADJECTIVE   A PLACE

   so they're not contaminated with toxic _____ .
                                            PLURAL NOUN

2. When it's time to plant, always _____ your seedlings
   VERB

   with lots of _____ so they _____ up big and
   TYPE OF LIQUID   VERB

   _____ .
   ADJECTIVE

3. Use organic fertilizer on your _____ , so the
   SOMETHING ALIVE (PLURAL)

   bugs and _____ in your garden stay _____ .
   ANIMAL (PLURAL)   ADJECTIVE

   That's what nature _____ !
   VERB (PAST TENSE)

4. Plants should be _____ in a/an _____ -house
   VERB (PAST TENSE)   COLOR

   to keep _____ and other pests from _____
   ANIMAL (PLURAL)   VERB ENDING IN "ING"

   them.

MAD LIBS® is fun to play with friends, but you can also play it by yourself! To begin with, DO NOT look at the story on the page below. Fill in the blanks on this page with the words called for. Then, using the words you have selected, fill in the blank spaces in the story.

Now you've created your own hilarious MAD LIBS® game!

IT ONLY LOOKS GROSS

ADJECTIVE _____

TYPE OF FOOD _____

VEHICLE _____

PART OF THE BODY (PLURAL) _____

ADJECTIVE _____

VERB _____

VERB _____

PLURAL NOUN _____

PLURAL NOUN _____

PERSON IN ROOM _____

NOUN _____

NUMBER _____

SOMETHING ALIVE _____

TYPE OF LIQUID _____

TYPE OF FOOD _____

VERB _____

EXCLAMATION _____

MAD LIBS®

IT ONLY LOOKS GROSS

So, let me tell ya a little somethin' about compost; it only looks

_____ . Okay, maybe it smells like _____
　　　ADJECTIVE　　　　　　　　　　　　　　　　　TYPE OF FOOD

that's been left in a/an _____ for too long, but that's
　　　　　　　　　　　　　　VEHICLE

because it *is* rotting organic matter and that does kinda smell like dirty

_____ . But after a while, old _____ food
PART OF THE BODY (PLURAL)　　　　　　　　　　　ADJECTIVE

turns into compost, and plants _____ it. It makes 'em
　　　　　　　　　　　　　　　　VERB

_____ better and grow beautiful _____ . Best of
　　VERB　　　　　　　　　　　　　　　　　PLURAL NOUN

all, composting keeps your table _____ from going to the
　　　　　　　　　　　　　　　PLURAL NOUN

landfill, and nobody, not even _____ , wants that. Some
　　　　　　　　　　　　　　PERSON IN ROOM

people call compost "black _____," and that's because it's so
　　　　　　　　　　　　　　NOUN

valuable. I mean, it's not worth _____ dollars an ounce like real
　　　　　　　　　　　　　　　NUMBER

gold, but it is pretty darn close. So, throw your old _____
　　　　　　　　　　　　　　　　　　　　　　　　SOMETHING ALIVE

skins in there and the leftover _____ from your juicer and
　　　　　　　　　　　　　　TYPE OF LIQUID

even your limp _____ . It all works, just _____ it in
　　　　　　TYPE OF FOOD　　　　　　　　　　VERB

the bin. _____ !
　　　　EXCLAMATION

From LOVE THE EARTH MAD LIBS® • Copyright © 2021 by Penguin Random House LLC.

MAD LIBS® is fun to play with friends, but you can also play it by yourself! To begin with, DO NOT look at the story on the page below. Fill in the blanks on this page with the words called for. Then, using the words you have selected, fill in the blank spaces in the story.

Now you've created your own hilarious MAD LIBS® game!

CLEANING UP

ADJECTIVE _____

VERB ENDING IN "ING" _____

ADJECTIVE _____

VERB _____

PART OF THE BODY _____

NUMBER _____

TYPE OF CONTAINER _____

VERB _____

SOMETHING ALIVE _____

NOUN _____

VERB _____

NOUN _____

ADJECTIVE _____

VERB _____

TYPE OF BUILDING _____

ADJECTIVE _____

VERB ENDING IN "ING" _____

MAD LIBS®

CLEANING UP

Two very eager volunteers are determined to clean up their very

_____ park:
ADJECTIVE

Monica: When I'm done _____ this park, it's gonna
VERB ENDING IN "ING"

look so _____ .
ADJECTIVE

Eve: Agreed! It'll be so clean you can _____ off the benches
VERB

with your _____ .
PART OF THE BODY

Monica: I'm going to put all _____ pieces of trash in this
NUMBER

_____ .
TYPE OF CONTAINER

Eve: Then, I'll _____ the lawn so that each and every blade
VERB

of _____ becomes as green as a/an _____ . This
SOMETHING ALIVE   NOUN

place is gonna _____ like a brand-new _____ .
VERB   NOUN

Monica: That's _____ ! Then, we can _____ the
ADJECTIVE   VERB

_____ until it looks _____ and new.
TYPE OF BUILDING   ADJECTIVE

Eve: Well, maybe we should stop _____ about what
VERB ENDING IN "ING"

we're gonna do and start actually doing it instead!

MAD LIBS® is fun to play with friends, but you can also play it by yourself! To begin with, DO NOT look at the story on the page below. Fill in the blanks on this page with the words called for. Then, using the words you have selected, fill in the blank spaces in the story.

Now you've created your own hilarious MAD LIBS® game!

UPCYCLED ART

ADJECTIVE _____

NUMBER _____

TYPE OF LIQUID _____

PLURAL NOUN _____

A PLACE _____

NOUN _____

NOUN _____

ARTICLE OF CLOTHING _____

VERB _____

NOUN _____

VERB _____

PLURAL NOUN _____

VERB _____

COLOR _____

PLURAL NOUN _____

VERB ENDING IN "ING" _____

NOUN _____

When I make my _____ sculptures, each wonderful piece is

ADJECTIVE

_____ of a kind. I only use recycled materials, like old

NUMBER

_____ containers, rusty _____, and other

TYPE OF LIQUID   PLURAL NOUN

discarded objects that I find behind (the) _____. Any little

A PLACE

_____ or bent _____ or even a worn-out

NOUN   NOUN

_____ can be part of my latest masterpiece. After all,

ARTICLE OF CLOTHING

you know what they _____: One person's trash is another

VERB

person's _____! Some people meticulously _____

NOUN   VERB

out their art projects in advance, but I like to trust my _____

PLURAL NOUN

and let inspiration _____ over! I often use _____

VERB   COLOR

paint to add interest, but only if the color is made from all-natural

_____. The hardest part of the process is knowing when to

PLURAL NOUN

stop _____ on new bits and pieces. Otherwise,

VERB ENDING IN "ING"

you may end up with a sculpture you can't get through your front

_____!

NOUN

MAD LIBS® is fun to play with friends, but you can also play it by yourself! To begin with, DO NOT look at the story on the page below. Fill in the blanks on this page with the words called for. Then, using the words you have selected, fill in the blank spaces in the story.

Now you've created your own hilarious MAD LIBS® game!

VEGAN FASHION SHOW

PLURAL NOUN _____

ARTICLE OF CLOTHING (PLURAL) _____

PERSON IN ROOM _____

ARTICLE OF CLOTHING _____

ANIMAL _____

CELEBRITY _____

PART OF THE BODY _____

PLURAL NOUN _____

ADJECTIVE _____

VERB _____

COLOR _____

NUMBER _____

SOMETHING ALIVE _____

VERB _____

LETTER OF THE ALPHABET _____

NUMBER _____

TYPE OF BUILDING _____

ADJECTIVE _____

MAD LIBS

VEGAN FASHION SHOW

Welcome to the Big Vegan Fashion Show, where we only use animal-

free _____ to make our gorgeous line of evening
        PLURAL NOUN

_____ . First on the runway is supermodel
ARTICLE OF CLOTHING (PLURAL)

_____ , who's looking good in a/an _____
PERSON IN ROOM   ARTICLE OF CLOTHING

made of fake _____ fur. Next, _____ is strutting
          ANIMAL   CELEBRITY

her stuff in an off-the-_____ dress made entirely
                PART OF THE BODY

out of recycled _____ . Looking for something more
          PLURAL NOUN

_____ ? Then _____ no further! Our next model is
ADJECTIVE   VERB

wearing our signature little _____ dress paired with matching
          COLOR

_____ -inch high-heeled shoes. And in case you were
    NUMBER

worried if _____ was used to make those shoes,
        SOMETHING ALIVE

you can _____ easy! This whole outfit is vegan with a
      VERB

capital _____ . Sure, at over _____
    LETTER OF THE ALPHABET   NUMBER

dollars, this outfit might break the _____ , but being
            TYPE OF BUILDING

_____ to animals is always worth it.
ADJECTIVE

MAD LIBS® is fun to play with friends, but you can also play it by yourself! To begin with, DO NOT look at the story on the page below. Fill in the blanks on this page with the words called for. Then, using the words you have selected, fill in the blank spaces in the story.

Now you've created your own hilarious MAD LIBS® game!

HOW TO CARE FOR YOUR CRYSTAL

COLOR _____

NOUN _____

VERB ENDING IN "ING" _____

ADJECTIVE _____

VERB _____

VERB _____

PLURAL NOUN _____

ADJECTIVE _____

ARTICLE OF CLOTHING _____

PART OF THE BODY _____

OCCUPATION _____

ADJECTIVE _____

NOUN _____

VERB _____

ADVERB _____

PART OF THE BODY _____

ADJECTIVE _____

Your new _____ crystal isn't just an old piece of _____ ,
　　　　　　COLOR　　　　　　　　　　　　　　　　　　　　　　　　NOUN

it's a mystical stone with _____ powers that will keep
　　　　　　　　　　　　　VERB ENDING IN "ING"

your spirits _____ whenever you need a little _____-
　　　　　　　ADJECTIVE　　　　　　　　　　　　　　　　　　VERB

me-up. You just need to _____ into the energy of your crystal,
　　　　　　　　　　　　VERB

and new _____ will open up all around you. You'll feel
　　　　　PLURAL NOUN

_____ and brighter just knowing it's tucked safely into
ADJECTIVE

your _____ , where you can always wrap your
　　　　ARTICLE OF CLOTHING

_____ around it in times of need. If you want, you can
PART OF THE BODY

even name your crystal after someone you admire, like your favorite

_____ ! Some people also like to name their crystals after our
OCCUPATION

_____ Earth. You can choose names like Gaia, Terra, or
ADJECTIVE

_____ Goddess. And don't forget, crystals perform best when
NOUN

you _____ them often! So, make sure you _____
　　　VERB　　　　　　　　　　　　　　　　　　　　　　ADVERB

polish yours with a little _____ grease and _____
　　　　　　　　　　　　PART OF THE BODY　　　　　　　　ADJECTIVE

intentions.

MAD LIBS® is fun to play with friends, but you can also play it by yourself! To begin with, DO NOT look at the story on the page below. Fill in the blanks on this page with the words called for. Then, using the words you have selected, fill in the blank spaces in the story.

Now you've created your own hilarious MAD LIBS® game!

LOVE THE EARTH STATS

EXCLAMATION _____

VERB ENDING IN "ING" _____

NUMBER _____

VEHICLE _____

ADJECTIVE _____

ADJECTIVE _____

VERB ENDING IN "ING" _____

PLURAL NOUN _____

VERB _____

ADJECTIVE _____

VERB _____

PLURAL NOUN _____

TYPE OF CONTAINER (PLURAL) _____

ADJECTIVE _____

VERB _____

VERB ENDING IN "ING" _____

PART OF THE BODY (PLURAL) _____

VERB _____

MAD LIBS

LOVE THE EARTH STATS

_____! I love _____ about how much

   EXCLAMATION   VERB ENDING IN "ING"

people are doing to help save our planet:

- In California, _____ percent of all _____ sales

                 NUMBER   VEHICLE

  were for _____ cars. California is "plugged-in" when it

           ADJECTIVE

  comes to being eco- _____.

                  ADJECTIVE

- More people than ever have started _____ off the

               VERB ENDING IN "ING"

  _____ when they leave a room. That sure helped us

     PLURAL NOUN

  _____ a lot of _____ electricity.

       VERB   ADJECTIVE

- One out of every two people say they always _____ their

                  VERB

  used _____ and disposable _____.

        PLURAL NOUN   TYPE OF CONTAINER (PLURAL)

  Recyclers are _____!

             ADJECTIVE

- More and more people are starting to _____ off their

               VERB

  water while _____ their teeth. That's one way to

        VERB ENDING IN "ING"

  have shiny _____ and _____ the world.

       PART OF THE BODY (PLURAL)   VERB

MAD LIBS® is fun to play with friends, but you can also play it by yourself! To begin with, DO NOT look at the story on the page below. Fill in the blanks on this page with the words called for. Then, using the words you have selected, fill in the blank spaces in the story.

Now you've created your own hilarious MAD LIBS® game!

EVERY DAY IS EARTH DAY!

ADJECTIVE _____

VERB _____

NOUN _____

VERB _____

PLURAL NOUN _____

VERB _____

ADJECTIVE _____

ARTICLE OF CLOTHING _____

NOUN _____

TYPE OF FOOD (PLURAL) _____

TYPE OF CONTAINER _____

NOUN _____

VERB _____

PART OF THE BODY _____

VERB _____

ADJECTIVE _____

MAD LIBS

EVERY DAY IS EARTH DAY!

I can't believe what a/an _____ time I had at the Earth Day
ADJECTIVE

celebration. From now on, I'm going to _____ like it's Earth
VERB

Day every day of the _____. I'm gonna _____ to
NOUN   VERB

school and turn out the _____ when I'm done using them.
PLURAL NOUN

I'm also going to _____ every bit of trash and start finding
VERB

_____ uses for old things. I could easily turn my used
ADJECTIVE

_____ into a dish _____! And better yet,
ARTICLE OF CLOTHING   NOUN

I can put _____ into a compost _____
TYPE OF FOOD (PLURAL)   TYPE OF CONTAINER

and wait for it to turn into a natural _____ for my garden.
NOUN

I also learned that I should _____ my mind, body, and
VERB

_____ because I'm part of this Earth, too. You know
PART OF THE BODY

what they say: Reduce, Reuse, and _____. Have a/an
VERB

_____ Earth Day, everybody!
ADJECTIVE

Download Mad Libs today!

stories on our apps!

creating wacky and wonderful

Join the millions of Mad Libs fans